Prism
of
FANtasia

Compiled by
Suhani Hanotwal

TGIBT PRESS

Published by "**The Great Indian Book Tour**"
Imprint : **T G I B T   P r e s s**
www.tgibt.com
email : prashant@tgibt.com

Title : Prism of FANtasia
Editor : Suhani Hanotwal
Copyright © Suhani Hanotwal 2022
All rights reserved

First published in 2022
First Edition 2022

ISBN : 978-93-93262-17-2

Index

Stories

Arts

Introductions

Poetries

"To my Moon and Stars"

On an autumn night, as I was looking at the sky,
You suddenly appeared to me.
I recognized your blue dress in the moon's turquoise colour.
You were there. You had always been there.

I went everynight to see this one moon,
But then, she showed me the stars,
Even dazzled by their brilliance,
I reached out my hand to touch them.

I started to always look at the stars.
I got attached to them.
I could feel so many things,
When I was with them.

Now, I look at the sky everyday,
Waiting for my moon and stars
To come to me everynight.

And everyday, the blue sky is beautiful,
Because of a moon and stars that we cannot see.

Arki

"Nobody knows it but me"
(SHINee's Kim Jong Hyun)

Only if I say,
Things are hard.
Only if I say,
It was a hazard.
Will it get better soon?

If I cry and say,
It hurts.
If I cry and say,
You are the one.
Will you be back soon?

If I call out to you,
Will you be there for me again?
If I call out to you,
Will you rush things up?
Or will I be left all alone,
Looking at the moon,
As if, no one cared?

Suhani Hanotwal

"Dangerous Criminal "
(Lee Taemin)

The most Dangerous Criminal
The most 'idea'stic person
Our Evil Maknae Taemin
The most cute person

Baby Cheese, Taemari, Taeminnie
He possess many nicknames
He is cute, naughty and sweet
Yet he is hot as volcanic flames

His dances moves are as sharp as sword
Also it is as fluid as water
He is one such idol in K-pop industry
Who stands tall forever

He is "Idol's Idol", idol for entire industry
He is King of K-Pop who reigns over industry
He is the Korean Michael Jackson
Who has created his own history

None can compete with him
None can surpass him
Taemin is and shall be the greatest Idol
None can replace him

Akash Ravi

"Idol"
(For all the idols)

You work hard,
Ignoring all your worries.
You act tough,
Knowing it pains a lot.
You give up everything,
To give us a lot.
Thank you all the idols,
For your devotion & love.

"Art"
(SHINee)

You're an art,
Pained by god.
Every stroke of your beauty,
Is created with warmth.
Imperfectly perfect,
Your existence is deep.
To ones who finds you immortal,
Is Shawols, who you love.

Suhani Hanotwal

"The stranger once I was"
BTS (Suga)

Lot of things happening around
Too confused to focus on one
Voices that came from within
Told me to hold on to the last hope.

Thought it was tough to handle
I guess it was just in my head
Closed my eyes, took a deep breath
Just remembered the stranger once I was.

Those fearless words, free spirit,
That pure smile, loud laughters,
Excitement to talk to everyone I saw

Wonder if I really was her once.

All alone, between the four walls
Not a single soul catching my eye
Too silent that my breath was too loud

It'd be better if there's wasn't any noise.

From too talkitive to too silent
From day to night, smiles to tears,
That's what I am now,
A complete stranger to who I was!!

Deeksha Shastry

"My Cheerleaders"
(BTS)

Why do I have the pictures of these seven men in my phone you ask?

Well those men gave me the motivation when I wanted to scroll my day away.

Why do I have posters of these men in my room you ask?

well, every time I look at them I hear them saying "you just have to make it to that day".

Why do I care so much about these men you ask?

well, when no one cared, and no one noticed, they became the best cheerleaders I will ever have.

Why do I choose these seven men over anyone you ask?

well, because when I wanted to give up they held my hand and told me to keep going, told me that they were proud of me.

Why I love these men the most you ask?

Well, when I was being judged by my family and society, they told me it's okay to be different and so I started to love myself more.

Why do I look at these people I will never meet you ask?

Because one day, I will meet these people and I will thank them for being the only

motivation and I will tell them that I made it.

- Raj Nandini Tak

"Fable of a Fallen Angel"

Like the ray of light peeping through the cloud
To me my life, you have endowed
I was a fallen angel with no memory
My wings as useless as debri

Embarrassed from the peculiarity
I hid myself in solitude
Yet you held my hand in singularity
And pulled me out of my desuetude

Meeting you was euphoric destiny
Like a bubble pop from my fantasy
All I shared was a feather from my wing
So did others who recognised your ring

Fascinated and captivated by your existence
We assembled wings with every feather
You soared to the sky with your persistence
Invigorating us with your blissful zephyr

Seeing you fly high was epiphany
Turning the world into a harmonic symphony
Oh! my wings too has its utility
I too, am a fallen nobility

Raising to a crescendo
Making me a bird without a shadow
You taught me the limit is the sky
From now on, together we shall fly!

Maanya Sogali

"The Sea's Voice"

In this moment,
our voices connect
and our spikes field becomes blue sky.

In this moment,
starts the esence of brightest ocean.

In this moment,
our biggest wave makes the darkness shine.

In this moment,
we sing by the sea,
Like a conch,being echo of their voices.

We,
the sun that never cease to shine for them,
We,
their lighthouse of hope.

And they..
They are our reason of still brighting.

In this moment,
We are notes sailing in this blue harmony,
from the bottom sea to the whitest moon.

In this moment,
we fly through the clouds.

With the strength of a diamond.
Where our song stops the storm,.
At this place with the stars shines once more.

Our SHINee World.
-TBLWR,@theboyinlovewitharose.

Jonathan

"A gift from God"
(SHINee's Kim Jong Hyun)

All these days without you here,
Is a little bit more than I can bear.
From now on, we'll be happy that you were here,
And carry you within us everywhere.

Every night you pass my window,
As I am sitting here with a coffee by my side.
Thank you for keeping me company,
When I was seeking for a companion.

And the midnight still finds me,
Writing poems like these.
You're too far from us,
Yet here, within us.

Suhani Hanotwal

"Incomplete Soul"

I wish to fly, with dreams so high
When things go wrong , it makes me cry
Perfection, strong are the things I try
I don't know why it proves me lie

Huh,
But I feel like ,

Loving myself hating myself
Why I'm not trusting myself
Loving myself hating myself
Am I completely losing myself

P.S – This was written as a confusion state which resembles my personal life until I met my biggest inspiration BTS …

N.GEETHIKA

"Flaming Charisma"
(Choi Minho)

He is as cute as Squirtle
As Hot as Charizard
Fantastic flaming Charisma Minho
As strong as blizzard

The strongest among the strong ones
The most handsome among all men
Every fanboy aspires to be like him
Every fangirl's dream man

The most passionate person
President of Shawol Fandom
He shines brighter than the sun
He possess immense stardom

The best soccer player
The most idol sports player
When he competes in the sport
Everyone knows that he's the winner

He's the ultimate person
The perfect man to look up to
He is the ultimate person
I want to be like him too

Akash Ravi

"S U N and its S U N flower"
(Mew Suppasit & Gulf Kanawut)

When the Sun goes down,
Its Sunflower bends its head.
But when the next day,
The Sun is up,
Its Sunflower, with a huge smile,
Looks up to his Sun.

A 'Sunflower' without its 'Sun',
Is only a 'flower'.
But when together,
The Sun and its Sunflower,
Shines brighter forever.

Though the Sun is in the sky,
And the Sunflower on the land.
Never thought, the Sun & its Sunflower,
Could love each other,
Knowing their destinations are different.
Still they look,
Only at each other.
Still their actions are dedicated,
Only towards each other .
And this makes them love, even more.

Though, they never met each other,
But their love have no boundaries.
Even if one day, the Sunflower is gone,

I know, the Sun is there, every morning,
waiting and hoping for its Sunflower to come,
Greet him and love him once again.

These words might not be enough to know,
How much the Sun & its Sunflower love each other.
But these words are more than enough to know,
That the Sun & its Sunflower will always be there for each
other, Forever.

Suhani Hanotwal

"Handsome moon"
(Kim Jong hyun)

When the child do not know
The meaning of death,
The elders comfort by telling
'Loved-ones turn into stars.'

And we grow-up thinking
Its true, even though
We know the truth,
It still comforts us.

But I came across a person
Who told all
He resembles Moon
Being himself a star.

His voice so healing,
His eyes full of emotions,
He talks about his life
And comforts others with words.

But one day, he left.
Leaving beautiful songs behind
Our Poet, our Artist
And became a **HANDSOME MOON**.

Divya Sharma. G

"The Essence"
(Kim Jong hyun)

As our love has became in your prize. The essence of this memory will remain to our last sunset.

You will never feel that frost again, if the warm heart of the sun hug you eternally.

You will never feel this loneliness,
Our warm friend will light the moon in the sleepless night.

In a methaporical world the spring blossomed despite the dark nights with a sun smile.

-You did Well Jonghyun.
I gift you my smile.

Jonathan

"Shine"
(SHINee's Kim Jong Hyun)

If you are the moon,
Let me be your star.
So that we can shine together,
Through our dark nights.

"Mood"
(SHINee's Kim Jong Hyun)

Surrounded by dark colours in a deep mood,
The moon is here once again.
With its stars twinkling,
Making a diamond sky.
A voice from the night sky,
Shining directly to my heart.
As if you were here, right next to me,
And nothing could do us part.
I've always been thankful to you,
For making my heart dance.
And whenever we fall,
You are there to hold.

Suhani Hanotwal

"The Almighty"
(Kim Kibum)

The Sassy king
The savage emperor
The great Almighty Key
He is our ruler

Fantastic Fashionista
Terrific Trendsetter
The great Almighty Key
Fabulous Forever

King of Variety Shows
Always the Best Ending Fairy
The great almighty Key
Cheerful Cherry

All-rounder Artist
Does everything the best
The great almighty Key
He's a role model to the rest

Handsome Human
Possess Pure Heart
The great almighty Key
Thank you for your beautiful art

Akash Ravi

"A little too late"
(SHINee's Kim Jong Hyun)

I did let you go,
Doesn't mean I am giving up on you.
I did let you go,
Doesn't mean I won't look up to you.

It would still be me,
Listening to you all day.
It would still be me,
Writing to you all night.

From the start, till the very end,
It has always been you and me.
Let us stay in this moment forever,
Because there were things I couldn't grasp.

Suhani Hanotwal

"The Notebook"
(Kim Jong hyun)

In this notebook of a thousand stories ours disappeared.

Each letter went with your memory,

Talking with the oblivion.

In the most perplexed way my memoirs are empty dress of

dependence.

Letter by letter is yours such a moment.

On this our chain.

One verse at a time,

I get lost in limbo.

One verse at a time,

Further away from myself.

In this notebook of a thousand stories ours disappears and my

freedom flourishes.

Every letter drags oblivion.

Every letter goes with you.

In this notebook of a thousand stories each point is a begin-

ning ,each comma is a breath.

Jonathan

"The Stars"
(Monsta X)

The time began with "seven stars",
Named as Wonho, Shownu, Hyungwon, Minhyuk, Kihyun,
Changkyun, and Jooheon.

They are the stars of my gloomy night,
They are the happiness shine bright in my eyes.

They are like seven colors of the rainbow,
Colors of happiness, can bear-off all the sorrow.

There are countless reasons for loving and to support them I have,
And a bond like family between strangers we share.

They are the stars destined to be in my sky,
They are the joy I was craving for in my life.

I owe them a whole bouquet of thanking,
For their hard work and the love they are providing.

And because of them I know me better now,
They became my own little world of bliss somehow.

This is how the time continued with "seven stars",
Named as Wonho, Shownu, Hyungwon, Minhyuk, Kihyun,
changkyun, and Jooheon.

Divyanshi Dixit

"Affection"
(SHINee)

Lean on us sometimes,
We will be there for you.
Even if times are hard,
Let us fight with you.

If one day,
You want to hold on tight.
Let us know,
We will hold onto you.

Even though we are miles apart,
Our paths cross each other's.
As if our stories were written,
From the very start.

"Not alone"
(SHINee's Kim Jong Hyun)

Your heart once again lied,
It stayed quiet even though it was hurting.
And when you were asleep,
I saw you cry.
If we can share our happiness together,
Let us be there with you during difficult times.
Or else, it would never be fair,
If we smile together & you cry alone.

Suhani Hanotwal

"True Best Friend"
(Kim Jong hyun)

A man with a beautiful aura
A man with a beautiful smile
A man as cute as sun-flora
A man with whom you can travel a long mile

A man with beautiful voice
A voice that's so serene
A man, that's every girl's choice
A man, creator of "Selene"
He is the man of SHINee
He is the lovely Jonghyun
He is the backbone of SHINee
The creator of all the tune

Producer, Writer, radio host
lyricist, singer and dancer
He possess many talents
He is an all-rounder

He is with us forever
He shall be a member till the end
He is watching over us forever
He is the true best friend

Akash Ravi

"Go as we Grow"
(SHINee)

Thank you for showing us,
Even though he is not here physically,
Still he is with us always.

Thank you for reminding us,
To remember and love him forever,
Like he always did to us.

And as promised,
We, never once forgot about our dino.
Because as we grow, we know,
it has always been 5HINee Forever.

Suhani Hanotwal

"The Best Gentleman"
(Lee Jinki)

Dubu Dubu the white angel
The Best Gentleman ever
Dubu Dubu the best vocal
Onew, the superstar forever

Leader of "Shining SHINee"
A man with the pure soul
His Charisma is as sweet as honey
The man loved by all

His voice is all blue
Always calm and soothing
All your problems disappear
The moment you hear him singing

He is clumsy, He is dorky
He is filled with Onew Condition
SHINee World is really lucky
To have Jinki as leader of Shawol nation

Thank You SHINee, thank you Onew
Thank you for giving us life
Every moment you make us feel new
Energise us in our every strife

Akash Ravi

"As you enchant"
(SHINee's Kim Jong Hyun)

You are like a candle,
Who lights up our dark path.

You are like a compass,
Who shows us the right path
when we are lost.

You are like our parent,
Because you've known us enough
to know our pains.

You are that idol,
Who is always there with us
least in spirit.

Suhani Hanotwal

""Pearl Aqua Emotion"
(SHINee)

Earth, fire, water, Space, Air
These are the five elements of life
Onew, Jonghyun, Key, Minho Taemin
They are the lifeline of Shawol life

They are the five diamonds
They glitter in the sky like stars
They are the cause of pearl Aqua ocean
They are our superstars

Knowing them has helped me a lot
Every wound of mine was healed
Knowing them gave me strength
Every difficulty of mine was sealed

Their words charge our life
It pushes us to do our best
Their actions teaches us
That everyone is unique and are best

I'm just a tiny droplet
In this huge, pearl Aqua Ocean
I love them a lot just as I love my life
Towards them, I possess deep emotion

Akash Ravi

"Angelou"
(SHINee's Kim Jong Hyun)

Even after 1000 years have passed,

I would still be here,

waiting for you.

I would still be here,

Giving you all my love.

I would still be here,

So you're all right.

Suhani Hanotwal

"Every Step Together, Forever"
(EXO)

These three letters make us go crazy
These three letters make our life easy
These three letters always glow
Those are E, X and O

Precious as water, fire and air
The members are very important
They provide us the motivation
In times of difficulty, they act as reinforcement

We are EXOL, we are always with them
We shall be with them in future
We shall go hand in hand
Every step, together, forever.

Akash Ravi

"Letter from afar"
(SHINee's Kim Jong Hyun)

To all the beautiful words,
I never said to you.
I gathered them in letters,
That I set on fire.
And watched the moon,
Floating up into the night sky.
And caused a chaos,
Among the stars.

Suhani Hanotwal

"Forever a Forever"
(Everglow)

Everglowing members
Everglowing songs
Everglowing visuals
Everglowing Dance

E:U, Onda, Mia, Aisha Sihyeon, Yiren
The 6 powerful idols of the group
Everglow is unique and distinct
It is not a normal K-pop group

Every song is filled with high energy
Burning like Hydrogen in the sun
The fandom 'Forever' is like sunflower
Which receives light from everglowing sun

"La Di Da", "Dun Dun Dun", "First"
Every song is unique and best in own way
Every song they sing has their own charm
It enthralls the fans in all way

Happy to be their fan
Happy to glow forever
Happy to know them
Shall remain a forever, forever

Akash Ravi

"You are the one"
(SHINee's Kim Jong Hyun)

You are the one,

I wouldn't mind losing my sleep for.

You are the one,

Who I can never get tired of talking to.

You are the one,

Who crosses my mind throughout the day.

You are the one,

Who makes me smile without trying.

You are the one,

I'm afraid of losing.

And the only one,

I wanna keep safely inside me.

"Ceridwen"
(SHINee's Lee Jin Ki)

To the one, who is the sweetest.

To the one, who owes the prettiest smile.

To the one, who loves everybody dearly.

To the one, who cares about others more than himself.

To the one, who comforts everyone with his kind thoughts.

And to the only one, who outshines others.

Suhani Hanotwal

"Everlasting Friends"
(Super Junior)

If there is a Hallyu Wave
They are the creator of it
All started with "Sorry Sorry"
As people realized the power of it

One of the greatest K-pop group to ever exist
They are super and yet not Junior
One of the largest group to ever exist
They are Super Junior

Leetuk, Heechul, Yesung, Shindong
Sungmin, Eunhyuk, Donghae
Siwon, Ryewook, Kyuhyun
They have come a long way

Super Junior is really a role model
They inspire in every possible way
They are our Ever Lasting Friends
They make our life as bright as day

Akash Ravi

"Goodbye with smiling eyes"
(SHINee's Kim Jong Hyun)

I had so much to say,
But I couldn't find ways to say it.
I had so much to show,
But I couldn't find the right path
that takes me to you.

You left us with those goodbyes,
With your smiling eyes.
As if it was meant to be,
From the very beginning.

"Only Moon"
(SHINee's Kim Jong Hyun)

When people say,
"My happiness is over the moon."
I get more excited.
Not because people noticed that I am happy.
But because even the people know we are each others
happiness..

Suhani Hanotwal

"Navaratna"
(Twice)

They are nine precious gems
Pure and Innocent as they are
They are the 9 stars who rule us
They are so close to us despite being far

Nayeon, Jeongyeon Momo Sana
Jihyo Mina, Dahyun Chaeyong Tzuyu
These are the 9 precious stars
Whom are cute, sexy, gorgeous, savvy

These nine precious and glowing stars
These are Navras- Nine pure emotions of a person
Seeing these girls, and hearing to them
You shall be able to experience heaven

They heal your wounds
They erase your pain
They give you strength
To get up and fight again

We are the proud Onces
To have TWICE as our idols
We are really happy to be alive
In the same era as our idols

Akash Ravi

"A friend by my side"
(SHINee)

I remember how it used to be,
When nothing else matter but you and me.
Music and our future dreams,
We are still a beautiful team.

I love the way you could brighten my day,
Make me forget the mistakes,
Make the pain go away.

Under the same sky,
At different places,
It has always been us,
Watching the moon from beneath.

"Your shield"
(SHINee's Kim Jong Hyun)

I wanted to protect you.
But it all happened,
As if it was meant to be.

Suhani Hanotwal

"데리러 가 *Kim Jonghyun*"

To love is to die
Role reversal could never get this fucked up.
In the midst of a storm I freeze,
Just to wish that maybe this will lead me to my calm…
You.
I know you've heard a lot of "Why'd you do this to us"
But I wish I had said "take me along with you",
If that's what will heal me
If that's what will give me more of you
Come take me.
I long each day to hear that all this was a mishap,
But no…
Life is a gamble
I'm running away from everything that reminds me of you
But I'm trying to find you in everything.
Tell Me What To Do,
If this is a game, Oh Lucifer,
Find someone else.
I wish I could abscond
To a place where I could set my thoughts out free
But here I am in a world without you.
Living in my own world of you.
To think that there will never be another second of you in this
world
Makes me wish everything was for naught.
Your boys had a comeback, Bittersweet.
To hear your voice,
You'd harmonize
I'm calling out for you
Listen close.
Who would've thought that someone like you would want to end

their lives?
Who would've thought that one day all my life would come crash-
ing down to
someone who's no more?
My heart
My mind
My soul
They're all lying on my bedroom floor.
Come pick me up,
I won't move.
Come take me home,
To where you've gone.
Wanderlust seems so wrong,
Come back baby.
Love wanders from daydreams to nightmares,
Taking me through river beds, sea shores and rose gardens…
So much beauty that I took in
And in a blink of the eye,
Everything turns to thorns.
Cold blood yet fragile forming slushes under my feet
This life without you I seek no more.
In your presence, this world failed you.
In your absence, my whole world is failing.
Dropping second by second,
Like the heartbeat of the sick
Each song,each phrase;
My conscience, a prick.
But love, I'd walk through these thorns all my life
Stepping on them with reminiscence.
Hoping one day I'd reach a place where I'd be strong enough
To sow seeds that would later blossom
Reminding every single person of that one beautiful soul
That changed millions.
Everyone places flowers at your stone,

But no, I'm not going to mortify you.
Those flowers will live in the name of you.
Why plant your death when I can plant your birth?
The world believes you're dead and that's because they've only
heard your music.
I listen to it, take it in with every cell that makes up my existence.
With every breath I take in,
I spell your name
Learning a language just to understand you,
If only someone understood you.
I might ink a rose on my skin
And that might be a part of you
That's a part of me.
But what part of you asked you to let go?
Even when you tried so hard
When you cried aloud for help
And no one came for your rescue
Although they heard?
Ships and tanks go for war
What's worse than a battle within yourself?
A battle that seizes the will to live
A battle so strong that not even someone with so much love like
you could
triumph.
Yours: Bloodshed and fears
Mine: Bloodshed and tears.
Who am I fighting against now?
You tell me, cause I don't seem to know.
It looks like maybe I'm now fighting the same war as you were
And if I lose,
Does that mean I win you?

Abhinaya Raju

Stories

A POISON
(BTS)

A poison, absorbed by an unexpected torrid bite, of extreme depth, veering into a prodigious world, devoid of all painful realities, whose freedom makes you forget the memories, dethroned by fantasies, imitated by dreams, including the sun, king of this universe, only lets appear his luminous portrait, having quite simply the choice, he's the one who has for load to satisfy the desires.

A poison, generating an emotion as beautiful as hideous, a passionate love, without venomous romanticism, without humiliating defeats, a divine story between beings never fallen in an embrace of human warmth, in a soothing embrace, unable only to hallucinate them.

A poison, loving, lost from all certain hatred, fictitious, almost turned into a drug, without admitting the power of the latter, more exaggerated than an obsession, than an addiction, equal to a need, a bodily desire.

A poison, tasty, chocolatey, sweet as sugar, juicy similar to passion fruit. The desire to gorge the body with it, to take its breath away, to break its soul, no longer living on blood, having flowed over the blade of the dagger planted in full passion, but living on the bewitching venom infecting the rotting wound.

A poison, full of joy, ecstasy, perhaps even too much. The viper having finished dancing to the sound of the flute, nothing could stop her. This amat of ease, of artificial euphoria, was compared to an attractive pain, pictorial or real, false by abstractions, true by its violence, filled by the goodness of these seven angels, whether fallen or pure, tempting in spite of reason.

A poison, colored from various fiery hues to arid ones,

changing the iris of the eyes to a purplish purple assimilated to the Red Rose, married to the Orchid, not seeing the world pale, nevertheless, a white purity, soiled by the hypocrisy of black Roses, infiltrated behind the petals of their opposites.

A poison, despite the sensation of its delights, become bitter with disdain, raising Aconites, dark violets, beautiful irritants, like sirens, bewitching by their celestial voices, they trap the carefree anonymous, coming to venture into this garden of Eden, not letting the Lilies prevail.

A poison, certainly somewhat toxic, by the invading thorns, discreet weapons within crystal beauties, by pretext of protecting them, but a remedy, not the most sincere, the most miraculous, would be to seize these Aconites, suffocating them with olive branches.

Write L'Arts V - Mariella

Love letter for SHINee - A Shawol's words

To our beloved SHINee,

I'm a Shawol, who starts her day with your tones in Etude House CF as my alarm Hence my day starts with you. I always go for shopping and end up buying all pearl aqua color things will come to my sight. This color gives me strength, like telling me we are here for you and with you, my beautiful Shawol family, whom I've gotten from you.

SHINee is more than artist to me. In my life, SHINee is my guide, my strength, my love, my hideout, my happiness, my comfort and most of all my home. The ultimate warm home, where at the end of a day I can comeback and rest. My day always ends with listening to your songs, no matter wherever I'm.

SHINee - my source of happiness and inspiration. After I was introduced to SHINee, you always motivated me from my personal to professional life. I got to know even though I'm a chicken in this swan's world, I'm still special, I'm special in my own unique way. I got to know there is always someone, who loves me more than I do. I got to know different is not bad, it's just different than the other. I got to know never leave dreaming to achieve what I want and hard work is another name of miracle. I got to know I'm stronger than I think. I got to know it is okay not to be okay too. You, my driving force, I'm forever thankful to you.

I'm really happy that our path have crossed in this time span and we became from acquaintance to friend to family, who receives love and light from each other.

Thus I've become your shining Shawol. A small light in your pearl aqua SHINee World ocean.

Hope this pandemic will go away soon and we can again meet on a beautiful day smiling together.

우리는 운명이 운명입니다 ❤❤❤❤❤

From Mousona, your Shawol from India

A Journey to the Keyland

Warning: All the the views, opinions, comments and people mentioned are real, they are definitely not fictional. Grap your drink and enjoy!

First Encounter

The very first time I saw Kibum, I realized that he is not an ordinary person. At first glance, he wasn't even the most handsome man in the World to me. However, when I heard him speaking, my heart lost its rhythm and it started to follow his body rhythm. It is so crazy to talk about this. If you're ready, let me tell you about my journey to Keyland. It sucks you're gonna love it.

Voice of love, it sounds so epic, right? Voice of love was speaking Gyeongsangdo satoori[1] when it touched to my ears. I was learning Korean as a matter of destiny. I wasn't so interested in Korean culture, music whatsoever at those times. I was learning French as a selective course at university. But at the second year our French professor left the school and the new French professor wasn't attained for three weeks. At the fourth week, they said I had to choose German or Korean. But the German classes was going on since last year but Korean was a new course. So, I thought that starting to a new language from very beginning is better than trying to reach up to the level of German learners. They were B1 level and I just knew something like A1 level German as I take it in high school, I wasn't even interested in it. It took just one second to choose Korean to me.

1. A local South Korean accent

Our professor was Korean and his Turkish was too cute. I liked the course at first but after learning Korean Alphabet Hangul, we started to learn grammar rules and some vocabulary and it was so confusing. So, I wanted to watch some Korean dramas. Because I am a Musical learner[2], and I thought that I can learn somethings by being exposed to the language. Then, I run into Drinking Solo[3] at times I was passionate about learning speaking and differentiating local accents. It was right after I watched Reply 1997[4]. It's already going so boring, sorry guys I warned you.

I decided to watch Drinking Solo after reading the comments about its being a drama about a bunch of teachers' lives. It sounded so interesting because I wanted to know about the life of my colleagues in Korea, even if it's a fictional drama. When I saw Gong Myung and Key I complained "Ah what is this, I thought it was gonna be teachers' drama, what are those guys now?" It wasn't so pleasant to see them at first. But Key distracted and attracted me so much that all the negative thoughts disappeared in a short while. Also, I thought they should write another drama about Kim Kibum character and his adventures. Nowadays I keep watching the drama I dreamed of. And it couldn't be any better.

2. According to the Howard Gardner's Multiple Intelligences theory
3. A TVN Drama starring Ha Seokjin, Park Hasun alongside Key.
4. A TVN Drama including so much Gyeongsangdo Accent (also known as Busan Accent)

Sparkles

Have you ever heard about Barney Stinson[5] and his theory about Suits? Yes, most of the women think that men look good in suits. I am one of those women.

There were many moments I thought that Key was so attractive while I was watching Drinking Solo. But the moment I actually fell for him was when he dressed up for his grandmother's birthday. I couldn't take my eyes off of him. He was shining brighter than a diamond. That was the moment I found out that I was the fish on the hook and I was so willing to be caught by him.

Those days I heard many people talking about Shinee and at some point, I said: "Who is that Shinee for the sake of God? What is so special about them?". I didn't know what would happen to me back then.

Descendants of the Sun[6] was also one of the dramas I watched when I first started to learn Korean. Those days I was just watching dramas to improve my Korean. When I was watching Descendants of the Sun, I thought "Hmm, the actor who plays the Doctor Lee Chiyeon[7] must be a singer, he sounds like a nightingale when he is speaking." Then, I searched on Google and found out that he is a real singer. I was so proud of myself for realizing a precious voice but I

5. A fictional character portrayed by Neil Patrick Harris and created by Carter Bays and Craig Thomas for the CBS television series How I Met Your Mother.

6. A KBS drama starring Song Joong-ki, Song Hye-kyo, Jin Goo, and Kim Ji-won alongside Onew.

7. A fictional character portrayed by Onew and created by Kim Eunsook for the KBS Drama Descendants of the Sun.

didn't bother myself to listen to his songs. Well, to be honest I wasn't interested in K-pop and I used to have prejudices unfortunately.

I was a big fan of the drama Fight for my way[8]. Thanks to my admiration to Kim Jiwon and Park Seojun's acting I've watched "To the Beautiful You"[9] and "Hwarang"[10], too. And I got to know Minho a little bit. You know there's an expression used to describe some kind of handsome man which is like a Greek god.

Choi Minho was a man like a Greek god to me. He was so "Wow", too hot to handle. But the one who made me want to listen to Shinee was Kim Kibum without a doubt. Deciding to listen to Shinee was the best thing I've ever done in my life, they changed me and my life in a positive way and they still do it. I owe many things to those five people and I don't know how to pay back.

Fangirling: Here we go again

When I was younger, I was a very dedicated fan of Jonas Brothers[11] and I was really good at it. Not only my teenage years but also my whole childhood years was spent by fangirling over some musicians, singers, bands and etc. But when I started to study at university, I felt like I should give up on being like this. I thought it was so childish. After that, I couldn't even fangirl around because of the

8. A KBS Drama starring Kim Jiwon, Park Seojun, Song Hayoon, Ahn Jaehong.
9. An SBS Drama starring Choi Minho and Sulli alongside Kim Jiwon.
10. A KBS Drama starring Park Seojun, Park Hyungshik, Go Ara alongside Choi Minho as Suho.
11. An American boy band consisting of real brothers: Kevin Jonas, Joe Jonas and Nick Jonas

hectic university life. But at my senior year I found out that the fangirl in me was still alive. And rather than being a kitty, she was a tiger now.

Shinee boys made me do the thing I thought I would never do again. I did the things I have never done in my life. When I look back now, Je ne regrette rien.[12] I have no regrets about being a fangirl for Shinee, and all the other people I liked before. At the age of 21 they brought back the beautiful soul in me and helped me to enjoy my life.

It is so personal to talk about this but I'm going to tell this out loud. When I met Jonghyun, I overcame a personal problem I couldn't solve for a total four years. It was really so hard to me and I could never tell that to anybody. But one night he came to my dream and told me "It's okay". For the first time in my life, someone told me "It's okay to feel like this.". Even if it was a dream, I was glad to have someone by my side and after that night my four-year-old night-mares have disappeared and I could finally sleep in peace without thinking that shit. I was so relieved. I am writing this while shedding my pearls out of my treasure chest. Finally, I felt like I can breathe and I am so thankful for this. Actually, when that case happened, I wasn't even a big fan of Jonggie but he was a savior to me.

When it comes to Jinki, whenever I see him smiling, it's like he reminds me of it's okay to smile even if the world sucks. When he looks up to the sky, sometimes I hate that I can feel him but I say to myself: It's a part of our lives and we should be strong. Jinki is the reason of my mental stability. When I see him smile, I feel like the life is still liveable and lovable.

12. A French song composed by Charles Dumont, with lyrics by Michel Vaucaire performed by Edith Piaf

Taeminnie? I want to burn all the world when someone breaks his heart. I want to wrap him up in a cotton wool. Like all Shawols, I am such a Motherwol[13] to Taemin. I even kept a diary when he attended to the military. My love and altruism have no limit for Taemin.

Minho-ya! Stop being that hot bish! God, you created Choi Minho to embarrass the angels that singing their own praises, right? He has a kind soul, he is handsome, he is talented. He is literally flawless. Ah, he is so annoyingly beautiful in and out.

Kibummie? Key? Almighty Key? The Captain Freak? Key-bam? Bumkey? The whole story is about him, what explanation do you need more?

One last word: Being a fangirl or fanboy is not something to be ashamed of. I hate that people think that we are crazy. No, you are crazy! There are many bad things happening in this World but why do you mind our interest in K-pop instead of changing those things? Why are you guys attacking us instead of thieves, scammers, rapists, murderers and all those real bad people? What's wrong with being a fan of a singer or a group of singers? Being a fan of art, music, and all those good esthetical beauties, is it really a sin, is it a crime? I don't understand those people who attack K-pop fans or any fans all over the world. For the sake of God, mind your own business and let us enjoy our interests in peace. I'm begging you! Please!

Let's get back to our journey to the Keyland. Sorry for interruption.

13. Motherwol means Mother Shawols, Shinee fans who are nurturing to the Shinee members

No Way!

Is it even possible to resemble a person you have never met before? I have had many "No way" moments since I got to know him. His reactions to the situations, his words, his way of doing things... I questioned that a lot: "Kim Kibum, are you me?". Once in an interview, he was talking about something he wants to research and write a paper about. The way he talks about it quite passionately was just as the same as I do at university canteen. I am not kidding; we are soul twins.

Most of the Korean people choose meat over vegetables as far as I know. However, when he was talking about the jeon[14] he likes, he said he likes zucchini.

I screamed because I was thinking that mine is zucchini and for a second, I lost it. He amazes me with every single thing he says.

One of my favourite dishes is Hummus[15] which is famous for being my hometown's local food in my country[16]. And the only dish I make and my ex-boyfriend doesn't like is hummus. Not because I make it bad, he just doesn't like it. When Kibum shared hummus in his social media account, I was the happiest person in the world. Just as his taste in food, his taste of music, the colors he likes, his hobbies, even the dish soap he uses is the same as mine. Of course, all of those are just coincidences but don't mind me. I am just a crazy person. He's not calling us 'Little Freaks' for no reason.

14. A fritter in Korean cuisine made by seasoning whole, sliced, or minced fish, meat, vegetables, etc., and coating them with wheat flour and egg wash before frying them in oil
15. A Middle Eastern dip, spread, or savory dish made from cooked, mashed chickpeas blended with tahini, lemon juice, and garlic.
16. If you want to know, it's Hatay, Turkey.

Forever Yours

Once I got to know him, I realized I can't live without him. Seeing him first every morning, listening to his voice everyday makes me feel alive more than any other thing. Sometimes I can't even believe that he exists. He is so amazing that he makes me think like: "Is it even possible to run into someone like that for real?". One day he is the most relatable person in the world, he is so down-to-earth; but the other day he is the Sun of the universe and I feel like a useless rambling meteor rolling around the Milky Way. Yet, that's so okay to be a meteor or a stardust as long as he lights up my world.

One of the reasons why I love him so much is his being so fair, honest and outspoken. He is so himself. He is so real. When he does or say something, he never fakes it. He hates insincerity. He is so natural. He isn't like anybody else, he is unique. He can astonish you with giving the rough edge of his tongue but at times he is the kindest and the most caring person exists. Sometimes he comes under fire for being too much outspoken but I admire him because he is brave enough to say what everyone beware to say. What's wrong with being honest and telling the truth?

Once in a while he makes me feel like: "Wow, he is such a great person. I wish I was like this, too.". He's definitely out of the general conception of being an idol. Of course, he sings good, dances good and does everything he's supposed to do (even the things he is not supposed to do) but what makes him so special is definitely his personality. I love him as a musician, as a singer, as a dancer, as a rapper, as a designer, as a songwriter, as an actor, as a good speaker, sometimes as a comedian, also as the father of Commedes and Garçons, as a stylish man, as an inspiration, as a reason to go on, as a reason to live for, as a nice human being, as a handsome man, as a beauty icon and all the things he is. I don't love him for just one thing or I don't love him just being a good-looking idol. I can't reduce him to just one concept. He is such an amazing person which is found one in a billion. I feel so lucky to get to know him. The all Shawols out there (or lockets or little freaks, whatever you guys call yourselves is not that important), you guys are so lucky to have him as your idol. Wishing him success for all his life might sound like a kind of pressure because you know there are many ups and downs in life and we are all human beings after all. So, I hope he lives a happy and healthy life and I hope he never forgets that there are billions of people who love him deeply and sincerely even if he doesn't know who we are, where we are or why we love him that much.

Dear our Kibummie, you are so much loved and we've always got your back, do whatever you want, honey! My heart is forever yours.

Nurjuly S.

Love Beyond Age

"Noona. Let's breakup." Saying this Taemin took his coat and stormed out of the house. Jiwon was stunned by his words and could not move. Tears rolled down her cheeks. She fell on the floor and cried. After storming out Taemin walked endlessly till he reached the park. He put his coat on the wooden bench of the park and settled down. The old memories of them flashed back. From first meeting on Fresher's day, Taemin trailing her everywhere, confession, Taemin waiting at Jiwon work place after his class, Jiwon helping Taemin during his last semesters, their 100th day celebration, celebrating each coffee dates and finally to the previous night fight. Why did they fight which resulted in breakup?

Jiwon was two years elder to Taemin. They dated each other like any other couple despite of difference in age. Everything went well until, Taemin got into job. Jiwon wanted Taemin always to be by her side. After he joined the work, she had to walk back home alone. She had to cook food for herself and also manage things by her most of the time. Taemin would find time whenever he could to spend with Jiwon. As days went by, Taemin became busy with his work and would rarely come home. This led to the start of arguments between them. They would not talk for days. Every time it was Taemin who would recoil by preparing various gifts and flowers for Jiwon. He wanted her to understand him and his feelings. But the fight from previous night made him think to give each other sometime and hence decided to breakup.

He wanted some lone time to settle it down. Jiwon longed for Taemin to give her another chance. As their life started to move on, they started to miss each other in everything they did. Jiwon thought his love is gone and tried to move on. On other hand Taemin was always there looking upon her from far distance. Day went by. One day he got to know about Jiwon moving to US from her friend. Friends organized a small farewell party for her. Taemin was observing everything from a distance. He had mixed feeling seeing Jiwon happy. On the other hand, Jiwon was forcefully smiling for what was going on around her. She was not happy from her heart. The decision of going to US was not only to achieve her dreams, but also to come out of the past. As party was going on Jiwon felt the presence of Taemin and searched around to find him. But he was gone.

Finally, the day of Jiwon's departure arrived. Taemin felt restless and he could not pretend to stay back anymore. He rushed to the airport to stop Jiwon from leaving. Jiwon was waiting in the lounge area. She stared at her phone screen.

"Taeminnie "

She wanted to bid him final goodbye. But she put her phone back to her coat pocket. Taemin reached the airport and searched for her here and there. He finally found her near departure gate. He pulled her into his arms and gave a tight hug.

"Please don't go." He said as tears welled up in his eyes. Jiwon wanted to hug him back. But she had to let go. Pushing him away she walks towards departure gate leaving him all alone.

"Jiwon-ah…..Jiwon-ah"

Two years later:

" Love "

Phone starts ringing next to Taemin's bed.

It was the first call which rang every morning from two years. Taemin answered the call in sleepy voice.

"He-llo"

"Hello. Good morning." Said a girl voice from the other end.

"Time to wake up Love."

"Hmm…ok" he said and the call ends.

After the call he wakes up, have bath, getting ready for the office, have breakfast and then set to work. From two years it was regular routine to him.

Soon Taemin's birthday arrived. He received a red tie as a gift from someone. Today the morning call went a little longer.

"Did you set a blind date for me?" he said as he pack his bag. There was a small giggle from other side.

"Ok…I'll be there after work.

"Don't forget to wear it" said the voice.

With the smile on his face he ends the call and set out for work.

End of the day, he prepare himself for the meeting. As he unfold the red tie, it reminds him of his last birthday with Jiwon.

"Wow, a blue tie."

"Mmm. They say blue color dominants interviews. As you are soon applying for companies. So I thought of gifting it to you." Jiwon said happily.

"Tie it then."

"What?"

"I want to see how I look."

With the small laugh she starts to loop the tie around his neck. Her eyes met his.

"Why are you starring like that?" she said with a shy smile.

"I LOVE YOU."

A noise interrupted his memories. 'Sigh' he started to loop the tie around his collar and it turns out into messy looking knot. However he did not care about it because he was getting late.

He reached the venue. It's the same café where Jiwon and Taemin had their first coffee date. A waiter walks towards him and calls out

"Mr.Lee Taemin"

"Yes"

"This way please." The waiter leads him to the roof top.

He enters to see the place decorated with balloons and flowers. The waiter left Taemin confused. A lady like figure turns around in the midst of the decorated balloons and flowers wearing a floral flare dress.

"SURPRISE!!!" she screamed while popping the pop. Confetti and ribbons showers like rain on him.

"Ji-Ji-won" his bag fell from his hand.

Two years ago:

Taemin pulled Jiwon into his arms

"Please don't go." He said with teary eyes.

Jiwon wanted to hug him back, but she had to let go. Pushing him away she walks towards departure gate leaving him all alone.

"Jiwon-ah"

It was first time Taemin called by her name. She tried not to look back. Before entering the gate she turns to see him for the last time. But seeing back view of him standing all alone as if his world was torn apart, she felt the pain in her heart. She ran towards him. She hugged his back and tears flowed.

After sometimes they held their hands and were sitting in the lounge area. The speaker above them announces the departure of US flight.

"Is it important to go?" he asked in low voice.

"Yes" she said shaking her head.

"Its only for two years. So I can apply for higher level after coming back here. Till then you too have time to settle yourself."

"I will feel lonely after you are gone." He said with a pout.

She laughed and said

"I will call you everyday. Even though I am busy I will never miss to call you. How about giving you morning call?"

"Really!!" he said in a excited tone.

"Mm.. really"

Taemin gave a small peck on her lips.

Jiwon pulled him closer and they kissed passionately.

They were interrupted by the announcement again.

They hugged and said good bye to each other.

Present day:

He ran towards her and gave a huge hug almost lifting her.

Tears rolling down his cheeks he said

"Thank you….. Thank you for coming back." He then kissed her.

Parting from each other he questioned

"According to my count, you were about to come back next month. But –"

Interrupting him Jiwon replied " I cleared everything early so that I can spend your birthday with you."

Looking at him thoroughly she smiled and commented-

"You look good. You have not changed at all."

Taemin looked at her confused

She gave a small laugh and moves forward to untie his tie. As she loops it around his collar, her eyes met his again the same way like the other time. With the shy smile she asked

"Why are you starring like that?"

"I missed you"

"I missed you too."

"I love you" he said with a smile on his face.

"I love you too." She replied with the giggle.

In this way they promised to stand for each other every time and stay happy.

Divya Sharma. G

ONE
KASH'S POV

"Kashhhh!!!get out of the road…Kash!!!!"this were my last words before my accident…yes a accident…although it's totally my fault still ressa my overprotective friend crused the driver…with her harsh words…Right now I am on the hospital and the sharp pain in my knees say that I really hurt myself…for him…

"Yah!! idiot what are you thinking huh??now it's good for you if you share those bullshit thoughts with me. And never ever think about him " after speaking those harsh words she gave me a disgusted look mixed with anger.

"I'm sorry ressa…I didn't do it intentionally…I mean I'm just lost in my thoughts " while speaking those words the hospital door opened.A very familiar face standing there…inspecting my wounds with his wolfie eyes…his eyes shows his guilty his panic…then he enters into the room...one drip of tear falls from his cheek…his eyes locked with mine…he observed every portion of my body…seems like the time stands still when those wolfie eyes met with mine… suddenly a shivering goes through my spine…suddenly some past events flashing in my mind…a sharp pain covered my heart…I deviate my eyes as I don't want to feel those pain..the pain which he gave me…the pain which breaks my heart…no,no I don't want to see him…

"Are you ok Kash?" he asked me with a worried look..

"Does it matters to you?"I replied sarcastically.

"Yes,that matters..now answer me" he replied in an angry tone..

"Ouu..then yes sir I'm perfectly fine..oh my God see ressa Mr.lim is how much caring about strangers.."I retort sharply.

"Sorry Kash.. I'm so sorry about the past events but please don't say that you're a stranger to me you know" his sentence cut in the mid way by ressa..

"Mr.Lim please just get out of here..you hurt my friend mentally and look she hurt herself physically..you are successful Mr.lim… now con you may leave please "ressa said in a firm tone.

"I'm sorry kash,I really don't want to hurt you..I'm so sorry…"after completing his word he swiftly walked out of the room..

"Strangers"," sorry", "get out" those words just banged in to my mind….ugh I want to accept his apology but what about my self-respect..No Kash no you worth more than this…you can't accept his apology…

"kashhhh…yahhh!!!!"my thoughts were cut off by ressa's sudden screaming…I rolled my eyes..look at her in disgust…

"What ressa?" I asked casually.

"did he really like you?" reassa asked with some hesitation in her tone.

"May be.."I answer her but actually I really didn't know the answer.

Two
CHANGKYUN'S POV

I'm just attending a meeting with my group members. But some thoughts still cross my mind again and again. I received proposal from my best friend Kash and I really like her too but I can't accept her. I mean she is good but she doesn't fit in my lifestyle.. I mean her status is not that much good..and I really don't want to loss my fans. I know I just engaged with the actress but I really don't like her. When ever I'm with Kash I always feels comfortable. I can tell her anything,ask her anything.. and she never makes me feel uncomfortable but I just can't accept her as my wife…the world can't accept her" suddenly my thoughts were snapped by a phone call. A familiar caller ID showed on my phone screen..i pick up the phone….

" Hello hyung how…" but I was cut off by the other person.

" Oh kyun…thank God you pick up my phone…hey did you know about the accident ?" kihyun hyung asked me in a worried tone.

"No hyung? Accident?" I said in a confused voice.

"Yes kyun actually…it's happened to Kash but don't worry Ressa admitted her to the city hospital and she said that now kash is perfectly fine so don't worry kyun ok?" he said but In a gentle tone.

After hearing those words I just lost my breath…..I feel suffocated…I can't think straight…only her face flashed in my mind….I just hang up phone, without wasting a second ran towards the hospital…I really need to see her right now… I really love her..I don't want loose her..she is everything…and I just a disgusting person… it's all my fault..I'm so sorry kash..oh God why this always happens to me….

Time passed

After the previous incident in the hospital changkyun sitting in his arm chair and deeply into his thoughts.

"stranger " now I'm just a stranger to her…it's painful…but I'm the one who hurt her first…the hate for me in her eyes are just unbearable for me.. I just can't live my whole life with her hate. I really love her..i really want her as my life partner but I can't accept her for my profession…and I don't deserve her..she is such an angle and someone like jooheon deserves her better whenever she need help joo is always there for her…and I always gave her hard time…I know she is the only one who cares for me..but I have no choice… sorry kash, I'm so sorry…

THREE
KASH'S POV

We are really share a special bond…for me it's more than friendship but for changkyun it's simply a childhood friendship only a friendship..but we both can't change the current situation… changkyun still wants to maintain a good friendship with me but I can't do that…I can't face the man who broke my heart, the man whom I love more than my self,the man who engaged with a another woman,I just can't,. I can't hurt myself anymore…

Suddenly the front door open revealing a man whom I really loved so much but as a best friend…Jooheon….my bestie…infront of whom I didn't care about my vulnerable state….he gives me the courage…give me the strength….who always there for me…who always give me the best advice…who always give me the first priority…who always ready to accept me….

"Hey joo, welcome back..so tell me about your shoot..how's it?" I try to avoid the eye contact..I know how's his expression right now..I didn't say him about the accident..I know how disappointed he is with that but I don't want to disturb his work…

"Yahhh! Don't chage the topic okay..I know what you're try to avoid but did you know how upset I am with that…you didn't tell me ?"

The disappointmen is clear in his face…the anger and concern both are mixed with his voice. I can't help but I feel so helpless..I don't want to hurt him…and some tears are rolled from my cheeks… oh my God I can't hold my emotions and like every time again I cried infront of him..

"Hey love, please don't cry I know what happened in the hospital. Ressa tells me everything. Don't worry. Everything will be fine." Now joo just sat in the chair comfort me. Suddenly his tone changed…now with more concern and gentle.

That's the thing I really loved about joo he never hurt me no matter how much angry he is. Still he try his best to understand me, understand my unorganized emotions. I know he love me, he love me more than as a friend and I know how much I hurt him when I cried for changkyun infront of him. I hate this but I can't hold my tears, and I really hate myself for that.

"Joo I sorry..I don't want to disturb you..i really have no intentions to hurt you" I muttered…my voice is cracked due to previous incident.

"You never disturb me love…and I know how you feel..But love you have to move on, changkyun is now engaged with someone else. " joo said while caressing my cheeks with his thumb.

"Joo now I don't think about him..I want to move on I want to love someone else, the one who love me too, and with whom I could share my feelings " I said with a confident tone.

And from the expression I can predict that my statement is lil bit unpredictable for joo, and I know that I still love changkyun but if I continue this I will only hurt myself and off course joo too.

"Are you sure about that?" with a shaky voice joo asked me.. his eyes tells how long he was waiting for this moment. His expression clearly reflects his excitement.

"Yes joo…I'm sure about that."

FOUR
KASH'S POV

This the very day,the day of my commitment, the biggest day of my life. Now I'm going to be someone's someone forever and I promise myself that I've never thought about my past , from this time I gave him everything yes he comforts me when I'm struggling with my emotions, my breakdown;Now that's my time that I give him myself, my love,my everything…my thoughts were cut off by the door knock. I see a person was standing in the door fame with a bright smile…

"Hey princess are you ready now ?? Let's go. Your groom is eagerly waiting for you." He said to me and flash a big gummy smile.

"Yes Shownu oppa, I'm ready " I said and starting walking towards him..before joining him I just looked at mirror adjust my wedding gown a little.

"Princess you're just look like mum..Now my princess is a grown-up women and going to marry her prince charming…Kash I'm so soo much happy for you" a tear rolled down from his eyes as he says that to me.

"oppa..I love you and always loves you the same…after mom dad you sacrifice so much for me and the truth never changed that you're my everything " I said with a cracked voice.

"I love you too princess and I'm always there to protect you."

After our liltle but heart warming conversation I gave him a tight hug then we both headed towards the main hall…

I was to nervous, I held oppa's arm..the peoples greeted us with their bright smiles and claps.

I saw my groom…standing on the stage and eagerly waiting for me…his eyes flashed a certain kind of nervousness…seems like the moment stands still when our eyes met with each other… I saw a full acceptance, a pure love only for me just for me…yes he's my groom, yes he's my joo…my jooheon, my husband…my future and my everything.

FIVE
KASH'S POV

"I do. Yes I accept Miss son Kash Mina as my dear wife and I promise that I never left you alone ." My thoughts are cut out by a cute voice..

"Mumma , look mumma daddy buy Minnie some ice cream " our son running towards me holding an ice cream cup in her liltle hand.

"Aww so daddy only brought you some where is mumma's portion " I pouted holding my liltle son in my arms.

"Well here's mumma's portion but why mumma always only gives hug to Minnie?" While saying those words he makes a fake sad face.

"No daddy Minnie loves you and Minnie give you hug" those words just melts my heart. Our Child is just like joo, such a good person with a big heart.

"Mumma Minnie make a friend today." he told me with a proud smile.

"oh really! where's he ?" I asked with some curiosity.

"He's over there can I brought him here?" and from his cutely nervous face I thought that's must be girl.

"Sure..why not?? Just bring her don't worry baby" just getting my permission he ran towards the play ground.

"So now did we planning about our next child ? " Joo teasingly asked me..off course he always tease me like this although he's still my bestie and my loving husband both.

"Yes off course but we really need to think about Min.." suddenly my voice choked.. I see the same face, the same wolfie eyes..my heart skipped a beat...I just can't think straight..it's so painful...now

I have everything..my life is just perfect…a loving husband a cute son..a beautiful family…then why he came back…he always breaks me…but now I moved on..no actually I moved on 9 years ago when I say yes to Joo..now I don't want to break his heart…now I really love Jooheon.. and I don't want to loss him….at any cost. I make sure that I get him out of our life. I hate you Kyun..I hate you so much…"

Jooheon's Pov

"Isn't he Changkyun? Yes he is. I know that's happens some-day but now I really don't want to loss her…Now she is not only my wife but also the mother of my son but I can't hold her if she chose him over us…I know how much she loved him…May be now I have to convince myself…" My thoughts were cut off by Min's voice .

"Daddy look here's min's new friend kyun uncle. And kyun uncle here's Min's mumma and Daddy." The intro is really cute.

"Minnie I told you don't talk to the strangers then why you talk to him? Don't you find someone at your age?" suddenly Kash scolded at Min her voice is so angry and that's enough to make Min cry. But never scold him. Is that for changkyun. May be.

"It's ok love. You scold Min and it's kyun love. He's not a stranger." I try to calm down her .

"Mumma I'm sorry"

Changkyun's pov

"Love?Mumma ? Daddy? So it's her son She chose Jooheon. Now she has her own family. Her eyes clearly says that how much she hate me , and I deserves this. But I'm happy for her atleast now she have a perfect life partner. I promise you Kash I never interfere in your life again " my thoughts snapped by a sudden scold. She scold Her son ? But why ? I know her very well that she never shouted at any one but why she did this right now ? Is that because of me?

"Sorry I don't want.." I try to say but she cuttr me

"what you don't want huh? You leave me when I need you and now you suddenly appear and try to be the friend of my son ? Look Mr. Lim I clearly warn you that stay away from my son and my family, and don't came closer to my son." The anger totally clear in her voice.

"Love, please don't be so rude with him. May be he wants to say something. "Joo try to convince her..but she didn't want to listen anything from me. Her hate for me is so much and I know the reason very clearly.

"No Jooheon. Don't insist her please…I don't deserve this. I really hurt her so much in the past. And I really apologize for that" I try to say but my voice cracked.. I tried so hard to hold my tears but I can't…I started crying and begged for her forgiveness. I really want to apologize for so long. I can't carry the burden anymore. At that moment I'm desperately wanted her forgiveness but suddenly I feel a pair of small hand around my shoulder try to hug me…I can't help but smile at his cute action…..Min is just like his mom dad.

"Uncle kyun please don't cry…mumma look you make him cry. Daddy uncle kyun is crying "

"No Minnie uncle kyun is crying because he felt guilty. Once he make your mumma cry. " I try to calm her but the child suddenly spoke.

"That's ok uncle. Min's mumma is so kind she'll forgive you but please don't cry."

"Thank you Min " then I gave him a soft kiss on his cheek.

"Hey kyun I forgive you please don't cry…" Now she speak but with a gentle tone in her voice.

"Really?" I asked in an excitement.

"Yes off course Changkyun she forgive you and now promise me you came with us for a dinner and we are really glad if you join us." Jooheon asked me with a warm smile.

"I want to but I have some work" I try to spoke hut I interrupted by an uncertain action of Kash.

"Yah ! Kyunie if you don't join us then I swear to God that I will kill you". Kash speak with a teasing tone
And at that moment I feel like I just found my childhood friend. That's the same tone what she used before the incident. And I really feel a huge load of the emotional burden fell off from my heart.

"Kash thank-you….and yes I join the the dinner party."

Jooheon's Pov

Her reaction towards changkyun clear my all doubts. Now she really loves me, and she never leave us. But I saw the guilt in changkyun's eyes…he just want her forgiveness…his guilt always chase him..and that's really hard to see…I know changkyun, he's used to be a very jolly person but now I'm sure that he really go through so many bad things..and I have to help him…atleast our son is able to make him smile and I'm sure that Kash also notice this.. I just hope that she forgive him.

Kash's pov

The tears are so heartbreaking..I know kyun. He never cries infront of anyone..but now he looks so vulnerable…the each words from his mouth is so painful…I know he's wrong at that time but now he's really guilty and I don't want to see him at this state…although he's my childhood friend and no matter how much I'm angry on him but still I care for him…a forgiveness is may be better than anger.

At the dinner table

"Kyun did you know Minnie and your taste in music is just same" Kash spoke with a chuckle .

"Really Min?? " changkyun asked with a qurious expression.

"Yes uncle kyunie min loves music " Min answered with a shy voice.

"Do you know what kyun Min really likes you produced music. He's a true fan of your talent" jooheon said with a cute smile.

"Then how's that if uncle kyunie be the music teacher of Minnie ?" changkyun asked in his deep voice

"Yahh!! mumma look uncle kyunie guide Minnie " Min said with a cheerful voice.

"Sure kyun it's a great idea " Kash says with a huge smile.

"Then it's final right ? " jooheon asked while sipping his drink.

"Yes..and I'm really glad that I get the opportunity to teach him". Changkyun said but suddenly Kash cut off him and spoke

"Hey! Please don't start again and I know you , so don't be so formal with us although we're friends now"

"No not only friends we're now family " jooheon added with a warm smile.

Sonia Ganguly

ARTS

Divya Sharma

Prapti

Prapti

Devi

Devi

Prapti

Prapti

Shakthi Devi Mezzico

Shakthi Devi Mezzico

Devi

Devi

Prapti

Prapti

Shakthi Devi Mezzico

Shakthi Devi Mezzico

Devi

Devi

Shakthi Devi Mezzico

Devi

Shakthi Devi Mezzico

Shakthi Devi Mezzico

Devi

Devi

Shakthi Devi Mezzico

Shakthi Devi Mezzico

Devi

Devi

Devi

Shakthi Devi Mezzico

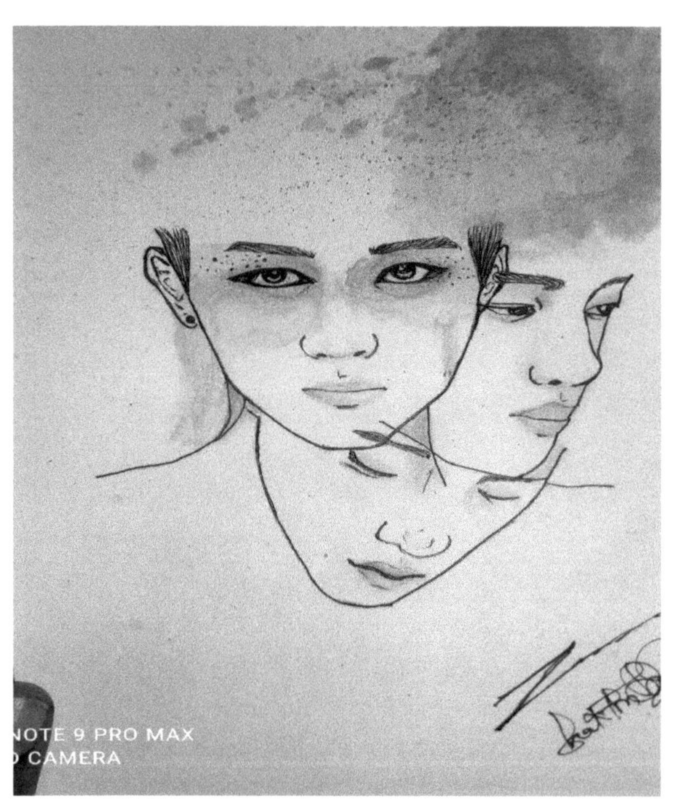

Shakthi Devi Mezzico

Introductions

Akash Ravi

Akash Ravi is a 27-year-old man living in Bengaluru. He loves writing poems a lot and has been writing as a hobby since when he was in Grade 2. He writes poems in English, Kannada, and Sanskrit.

It was in 2017, his friends introduced him to Korean World. They suggested him to watch K-Drama and his first K-Drama was "My Girlfriend is Gumiho". From there the journey started. His first K-pop group was SS501. Park Jung Min's "Not Alone" and SS501's Boys Over Flowers OST "Because I'm Stupid" pulled him to the world of K-Pop. However, he realised that they are disbanded. Then "Stand by Me" song from the same drama made him enter a new world called SHINee World. Since SHINee is like SS501 in many ways, he started seeing SS501 in SHINee and gradually fell in love with them. From then he started following many other groups like TWICE, Super Junior, EXO, EVERGLOW, Girls' Generation (SNSD), Dramcatcher. But SHINee shall remain as his ultimate group forever. To express his love for them, he has contributed his share of poems. Hope you all enjoy it.

Abhinaya Raju

India

Abhinaya Raju is a 22 year old Medical and Psychiatric Social Worker who is extremely passionate about making a change in the world and in the lives of others, no matter how miniscule. Music is her love, survival kit, coping mechanism and all words that describe "the reason I'm here". She is also an active advocate for various issues/purposes like Women Empowerment/Rights, LGBTQIA+, Mental Health and other social issues. A fangirl by nature, she loves spreading and giving love to her fullest potential. Oh and, Treat People With Kindness!

She belongs to SHINee World and SHINee was the reason she got into Kpop. The other band I stan is SuperM which was of course because of our little Taeminnie. She also loves Exo, NCT and WayV. Her ultimate stan biases are Choi Minho, Bhyun Baekhyun, Ten Lee and Mark Lee. She was introduced to Kpop by Jonghyun and that was also how she found SHINee. She fell in love with them because of their aura and personalities. Watching their interviews and funny moments was how she got into them before she even heard their songs, and that is why she believes she loves them more than she could fathom or articulate. She describes it as like coming back home, after a long day of nothing but a hectic life of having to hold on. But the home is SHINee. Abhinaya also loves them for how they love Shawols and how they always show it. She has gained so many friends from the fandom that she will cherish for a lifetime. Her ultimate bias is and will always be Choi Minho. And yes, Jonghun, her love, for whom she is forever grateful for.

The poem that she wrote: " 데리러 가 Kim Jonghyun " is for and about SHINee's Jonghyun. She wrote this a few months after he passed. This holds a lot of meaning in her life because he changed it drastically. She is a survivor of PTSD and it was caused due to the death of someone she knew. This particular incident occured in March 2017 and when December 18th 2017 happened, she went numb. Her PTSD was over the roof. In the beginning of 2020 she battled hallucinations and by the end of the year, she came out healed and stronger. Through her mental health journey, she has become such a stronger and evolved person, and for that she thanks her beloved Jonghyun. Everytime she looks at the Moon, she knows he's here to check on her. She will forever and always love him, in love and in death.

Instagram: theinkedthought
Twitter: 1Dxshinee_

Deeksha V Shashtry

Deeksha V Shastry is a 19 years old graduate student from commerce field. She found herself keenly interested in poetry writing and literature. She wrote this poem to express her thoughts about the changes she underwent after happenings of one of the greatest events of her life. Life isn't easy on anyone. So wasn't for her too. The negative impact on her mental health from the hardships she went through was a lot. A born extrovert natured girl had changed to a loner. That's when BTS paved the way for her in mental upliftment and to become a better person. She grew up as a positive and rational thinker.

"Love yourself" and "Speak yourself" campaign by BTS in collaboration with UNICEF helped Deeksha accept herself and love herself. And today, she stands as an unafraid pragmatist and proud ARMY.

This work of her's is dedicated to BTS who stood by her at all times and constantly motivated her.

Devi

Devi is a 23 years old girl from Bangalore, India. She has completed her Master's in Commerce from Nagarjuna College Of Management Studies.

She finds her soul dancing and drawing around her biggest inspiration, that is, her favourite Korean - pop band BTS.

Currently, she's enjoying her days fangirling BTS which helps her erase all her worries and find only happiness.

She's an Army since April 2020. 'Boy With Love' choreography impressed her with their attractive dance moves.

Their dedication, friendship and love towards each other and towards their fans made her realise how much she adores them. She finds herself motivated and full of energy whenever she looks at them. When LOVE YOURSELF campaign of BTS started, it really touched her heart and made her love herself more and encouraged her to speak for herself again.

She's really thankful to Suhani, the organiser of this project, for giving her this great opportunity to express her feeling and emotions in this short paragraph.

Because BTS deserves it, Devi is ready to work for them day & night.

Hope people reading it will enjoy all our works and will support & love us a lot.

Thank you.

Divya Sharma

Divya Sharma G from India, likes to express her views and feelings through poetry and her imaginations through stories in words. She loves doodling and various other creative things too. She loves SHINee who pumped her back to life. Their excellent songs and legendary performance made her to fall in love with them forever. SHINee inspired her in many ways. She is currently a home-tutor and a story-writer under a pen name. Her dream is to become a small-business entrepreneur and to help people who need emotional support. Hope you like her work and enjoy this book.

Divyanshi Dixit

Divyanshi Dixit is a 17 years old girl who really loves MonstaX and have a great interest in Korean culture. She finds MonstaX a highly influential and talented group with incredible singing and dancing skills. MonstaX has always been kind and generous, not only to their fans but also to whom so ever they meet.

MonstaX is the reason she got to know how beautiful Korean culture is and they are the basic grounds behind her exploring many new things.

Divyanshi is currently studying fashion designing and you will soon find her with her own famous brand.

If you see her somewhere, do not miss an opportunity to meet her cause she's the sweetest soul you'll ever see.

Hope you will enjoy her works shared as well as appreciate the creativity and handwork done for this book.

Thank you.

Geethika

Geethika is 22 years old girl from Hyderabad, India. She is undertaking graduation in K.L University .

She loves to do dancing and recently found her interest in writing poems, lyrics and writing fanfictions She known the meaning of life when she came to know about biggest boyband BTS in 2018.

She is thankful to devi and suhani who had included me as a part of this wonderful opportunity.

Hope people who go through this will love and support us .

Thank you.

Raj Nandini Tak

Raj Nandini Tak is a 18 years old girl who lives in India. She discovered K Pop through EXO and has fallen in love with the famous Boy band, and after going deep into the world of K pop and different fandoms she found her comfort space in BTS, so she is now an ARMY.

She is a psychology major student and soon to be organisational psychologist, she is determined to have a positive and mentally stable society for the future generation. She also holds a place in her heart for Animals around the globe and is determined to contribute in saving our Mother Nature by encouraging sustainable development.

She believes we are all going to be judged, so do whatever you love and if you are having a bad day always remember" 100 bad days=100good days". I hope anyone who reads this book keep in mind the book will be your get set light for a good day.

Jonathan M.L.

Jonathan M.L is a 22 years old guy who loves SHINee since the first moment he met Jonghyun. He felt in love due the Jonghyun's poetry ,there he found his inspiration and a new life style was born.

Now he is poet and he even created a popular poetry page named @shawolboy.uwu (on instagram) and is writting a physical book.

He is nutrition studient and soon psychologist,he loves to help others with emotional empathy even over him.

His dream,help those who didnt receive other's hope.

I hope you like it.

Please, enjoy this book.

Maanya Sogali

Maanya Sogali is a 24-year-old poet, lyricist and Korean language interpreter. She is from Bengaluru, India. She has completed her engineering in Biotechnology from Dayanandasagar college of Engineering.

She is currently an event manager by the day and a fangirl by night. She has worked enormously in establishing Korean interests in the city of Bengaluru. She is also a composer/producer under a pen name that no one knows about. If you find out, let us know! If you are further curious, you will need to wait for her next work!

Mariella

Mariella is a 16 years old girl who lives in France. She discovered K-Pop and has fallen in love with a famous Boys band, BTS, so, of course, she has become an ARMY.

Thanks to this successful band, she found a new universe where she can break free of all pressures of life to become stronger and braver. Now, she's not afraid anymore, and keeps getting better every day.

Mariella is passionate about arts, especially drawing and writing. She has been drawing since she was a kid, but she began writing not long ago, starting with some poetic texts before writing some novels, especially horror and creepy but also some platonic passion novels.

She created her own world through her writings, expressing her feelings, her thoughts, or simply her little world, more or less pretty, because passion is pain, but such an amazing pain, which makes you sick but lively at the same time.

That's what she wants to share, her passion for arts, with perhaps her personality at the same time.

BTS inspired her so much, finding models to follow which encourage her to live how she wants to live this pretty life which has to be lived with this kind of pain, passion.

She doesn't draw, write, paint, express, for a certain pleasure, but for her freedom of expression and for the beauty of art that she admires for its diversity.

Mariella has one motto, more or less complicated to understand : « Live your life like tomorrow doesn't exist, but be patient because tomorrow will be better. ». If she explains it, she will say that you have to be concentrated with the present, because you have the power on it, but you have to be patient because the future can hide some pretty things. Linking together, it's what you're doing now will give you a great gift.
Sincerely thanks.

Mousona Biswas

Mousona Biswas is a Software Engineer, who has a deep interest in Korean culture and the country South Korea. She was attached with it from her avid attraction towards Kpop band SHINee.

SHINee and their music and ideologies made her follow the path "Fans are the reflection of their idols." As she strongly believes in this, she is continuously working towards to be better and to help others. She has been involved in various NGO activities (both human/animals and nature) since then.

Often an author by interest Mousona wishes this book can bring the love from different colors and flavors of Kpopsickles to their idols and can be the loving memories to many.

Nurgul Seven

Nurgul Seven was born in İskenderun, Turkey in 1998. She was interested in books since her early childhood period. When she was a high school student, she was chosen as the bookworm of the school
and got a prize. She started to be interested in foreign languages and cultures at her teenage years. Learning English, she also started on learning Hindi and Urdu, falling under the spell of magical Bollywood World. She wrote her first and the second poetry books at her first year of university.

Seven joined Drama Club of University, she took courses about dramatic writing. Studying English Language Teaching at Dokuz Eylul University, she studied French for two terms and also Korean for two terms. Although she started to learn Korean due to the course credits, she fell in love with the Korean Language and Culture. After the graduation she proceeded to study Korean. She took part in Korean speaking contest held by Korean Culture Center of Embassy of the Republic of Korea.

Thanks to all these incidences, she run into SHINee and SHINee World which have changed her life afterwards. As the autumn comes and the leaves fall, with the first snow hearts fall for, as the spring comes flowers bloom, as the sun comes up and all get warm; the destiny flow like a river and brought them together. And the journey has begun…

Shakthi Devi Mezzico

Shakthi Devi Mezzico is a multi-lingual artist and a professional make-up artist. She hails from Chennai, India. She is quite a multi-faceted who holds a bachelors degree in music, yoga and A Diploma in Make up. She is currently in her gap year to relax and recharge after nearly 2 decades of worldly pursuits. She lights up the world with her contagious bubbly smile besides singing , painting , playing instruments and practicing her artistry skills. She is looking forward to hail as a glorious musician and win that Oscar someday.

Suhani Hanotwal

Suhani Hanotwal is an 18 years old girl who's currently living in Jaipur, Rajasthan. She debuted as a writer & editor of the book "BREATHE UNDER THE MOON."

Apart from that, she has also worked on another book "The early bird."

Suhani enjoys reading Romantic Comedy but adventure never leaves her bookworm head either. She is a hardworking and determined person who finds perfection in her imperfections. Suhani's major inspirations that got her into the world of writing is her favourite Korean - pop band SHINee and of course, it won't be possible without her parents, who have always supported her and her friends, who always tried to keep her sound sane.

Suhani believes that we all have different ways to express our gratitude, emotions and love for someone. And this is the most beautiful way, she found to express herself. And not only her, many others found their happiness in poetry, writing and arts. So, existence of this book in itself means a lot, not only to her but to each and every person who's attached to it, directly or indirectly.

Suhani is someone who creates her own mottos and boundaries, and there is something that never allows her to keep her mind in a single direction. Her room is full of books of all genres and each line has guided her to a new world.

Suhani resembles to each & every quote that she looks upto and her first quote that she wrote herself fits her perfectly :

"Write a book that you want people to read,

Draw an art that you want people to see,

Tell a story that you want people to listen,

And do everything you can, so that the world looks up to you."

Hope each and every person reading this finds their inspiration out of Suhani's work. And not only hers but any person who worked on this project on screen or off screen. Living with this motto "We are the different colours of rainbow bound together to shine like Light." she wants each and every person to find their happiness in whatever they do. All the very best.

Thanks & Regards.

Soonia

So it's all started with the girl named Soonia From India who has fallen for a 7 member korean boy band Monstax…and eventually become a loyal monbebe…she always have been heard about kpop and kdramas but never ever shows any interest but it all started when an interview catches her attention…and that's the interview of these boyband MonstaX, and for the first time she just listened to their songs and that's the beginning…then she started searching for the members and one after one song she's just fall for them harder…and that's how she becomes a Monbebe, Our Monstax's Monbebe. Sincerely thanks